I0159779

THE HIDDEN CHRIST: TYPES & SHADOWS

VOLUME 2 – SACRIFICES AND OFFERINGS

COMPILED BY HAYES PRESS

Published by:

HAYES PRESS Publisher, Resources & Media,

The Barn, Flaxlands

Royal Wootton Bassett

Swindon, SN4 8DY

United Kingdom

www.hayespress.org

If you enjoy reading this book and/or others in the series, we would really appreciate it if you could just take a couple of minutes to leave a brief review where you purchased this book.

CHAPTER ONE: THE BURNT OFFERING

Though the early chapters of the book of Leviticus might appear to be difficult and dry to less experienced students of the Bible, yet to those who meditate upon their shadows are disclosed some of the very precious truths that relate to the Person and work of the Lord Jesus Christ. In the offerings of this book this is particularly true.

In this opening chapter, we draw attention to the burnt offering, that among the offerings with which God commences, and that in which, as is generally accepted, we are presented with shadows of Christ as He gave Himself to God as an Offering and a Sacrifice for an odour of a sweet smell.

Firstly, we note the opening words of Leviticus 1. "And the LORD called unto Moses, and spake unto him out of the tent of meeting" (verse 1). Here we find the LORD in His house, a house that had been built both as to material and design in agreement with the divine requirement. God was the Architect, but the materials, the craftsmanship and the assembling were the responsibility of men and women who learned the will of God and carried it into effect. This certainly has its voice for us today.

Attention has frequently been drawn to the contrast between God's speakings here and those on Mount Sinai. There are no terrors here of a mount that might be touched, and that burned with fire, and ... blackness, and darkness, and tempest, and the sound of a trumpet, and the voice of words ... and so fearful was the appearance, that Moses said, I exceedingly fear and quake. God has taken up His place over the mercy-seat between the cherubim, and in grace and mercy He can communicate His will for His people through His servant Moses. Still, be it remembered, He is always the "thrice holy" God, and approach to Him must always be marked with that reverence and godly fear which are due to Him before whom the seraphim veil their faces and their feet. Leviticus 10 makes very clear that presumptuous approach will be met with devouring fire.

The worshipper who came to God could bring his oblation from the herd, the flock, or the turtledoves and pigeons. This was a divine provision to meet the condition of the offerer; and it speaks to us of varying levels of understanding and appreciation of the Person and work of Christ. All do not have the same spiritual attainment, but it's pleasing to know that the LORD is willing to accept from us "according as a man hath, not according as he hath not."

"If his oblation be a burnt offering of the herd, he shall offer it a male without blemish." The male of the herd was the highest in value of the offerings shadowing Christ. Whether from herd or flock, the burnt offering must be a male, and so the bullock speaks of the Lord Jesus in the highest aspect of His work on the cross of Calvary. While it is preciously true that Christ died for our sins and trespasses it is not this that is set out in the shadows of the burnt offering. Rather it is Christ who came forth to do the will of God, going up to the cross to give Himself in sacrifice to God. It has been fittingly said that the will of God included giving Himself to save sinners, but the type in the burnt offering, though atonement is made, does not raise the matter of sin, it is a sweet savour offering ascending as incense unto God.

What is of particular delight to the offerer is that he has acceptance in the oblation. "It shall be accepted for him." "He shall offer it at the door of the tent of meeting, that he may be accepted before the LORD" (verses 3,4). Perfection marked the offering, and the worshipper as he stood by the altar could rejoice to know that he stood before God in that perfection. In a loftier sense today we who lay our hands on the head of our Victim can rejoice that "He hath made us accepted in the Beloved" (Ephesians 1:5 KJV). In this connection we read, "as He is, even so are we in this world" (1 John 4:17). If this were more fully apprehended how our love for Him would be increased! What room is there for fear, as John writes of it, when we realize that all the perfections of Christ are reckoned unto us? He has been made unto us "wisdom from God, and righteousness and sanctification, and redemption." All that God could wish to find in His people He finds as He sees us in Christ our great Burnt Offering. Doubtless a similar truth is expressed in the word of God through Balaam concerning Israel, "He hath not beheld iniquity in Jacob, neither hath He seen perverseness in Israel" (Numbers 23:21).

Before we look into the death of the victim in Leviticus 1 let us note the importance of the command, "he shall offer it at the door of the tent of meeting" (verse 3). There at the door of God's House was His altar, and the Israelite was enjoined not to offer his oblations elsewhere. There was one God, one House, and one altar. Alas, that Israel failed to observe this command! "Though I write for him My law in ten thousand precepts, they are accounted as a strange thing," said God; and, "Because Ephraim multiplied altars to sin, altars have been unto him to sin" (Hosea 8:11,12). The truth concerning a Place, a Sacrifice, and a Priest calls for our close attention.

"He shall kill the bullock before the LORD: and Aaron's sons, the priests, shall present the blood, and sprinkle the blood round about upon the altar ... and lay wood in order upon the fire." We should note that the blood of the burnt offering victim was not taken inside the holy place. Only that of the sin offering was taken inside, in which case the body of the victim was burned without the camp in a clean place. There in the sight of the offerer the blood was applied, and we can think of him like ourselves as we sing that verse of the hymn:

"We hear the words of love,

We gaze upon the blood,

We see the mighty Sacrifice,

And we have peace with God."

It has been said, "The burnt offering is but the unclothing of the blessed Christ of God, revealing Him to our gaze in these shadows as God sees and knows Him." This is beautifully true, and the first matter mentioned after the sprinkling of the blood is, "he shall flay the burnt offering, and cut it into its pieces." The removal of the skin, and the severing of the pieces was the operation of the knife in the skilled hand of the offerer. The sons of Aaron, the priests, laid the head, and the fat, in order upon the wood that was on the fire which was upon the altar. The inwards and the legs were washed with water, and the whole was burned on the altar, for an ascending offering, and for a sweet savour unto the LORD. How striking that the Holy Spirit mentions in particular the head! The head being the seat of the mind and thoughts, which find expression in the will, takes our thoughts to Him who said, "I delight to do Thy will, O My God; yea, Thy law is within My heart."

The lovely story given us concerning Christ in the New Testament reveals how completely the will of the Lord Jesus was subject to the will of His Father. The scene in Gethsemane comes readily to our mind. There, faced as He was with the ordeal of the cross, we hear Him say, "Howbeit not what I will, but what Thou wilt" (Mark 14:36). He could say, "I can of Myself do nothing ...

because I seek not Mine own will, but the will of Him that sent Me" (John 5:30).

The fat was next placed on the altar. Here we are caused to consider the inner perfections of God's beloved Son, those hidden energies, His intrinsic worth. David cried, "Behold Thou desirest truth in the inward (covered, concealed) parts." As the fat was placed on the altar God saw the shadow of His loyal, devoted Son, in whose heart was the law of God. He always did the things that were pleasing to His Father. His meat was to do the will of Him that sent Him, and to accomplish His work.

It was He who could say, "Judge Me, O LORD, for I have walked in Mine integrity, I have trusted also in the LORD without wavering. Examine Me, O LORD, and prove Me; Try My reins and My heart. For Thy lovingkindness is before Mine eyes. And I have walked in Thy truth" (Psalm 26:1-8). As we view the head and the fat on the altar we think of the mind of Christ and the heart of Christ, that mind which was so lowly that He stooped down from the throne of God, right down to the death of the cross: that heart which throbbed with an attachment to His Father which is beyond all human comprehension. As the fat was all for God in the offerings so we judge it tells of that which God found in His Son, a depth of delight which was infinite, which God alone could appreciate. Would to God that in our case as servants of God our minds and hearts were more in unison in the thoughts and ways that give Him pleasure!

The inwards and the legs were washed with water and then put on the altar, and thus the whole of the animal was offered unto God (the skin excepted, which was given to the priest). This washing of inwards and legs brings the type to agree with the great Antitype, who was ever clean both inwardly and outwardly before His God and Father.

The legs cause us to trace afresh the pathway which He trod. There was no journey too great or difficult, wherever the will of God lay He was ever ready to go. If it were to meet a poor leper, touch him, and cleanse him; if it were to show pity and power towards a widow whose son was on the way to burial; if it were to give His back to the smiters, and His cheeks to them that plucked off the hair-wherever His Father's will lay He was ready to run in the way of His commands. Lovely are His words in John 14:31, "But that the world may know that I love the Father, and as the Father gave Me commandment, even so I do. Arise, let us go hence."

All these pieces were laid upon the wood in order upon the fire, and the fire fed upon the sacrifice all through the night, and throughout the day. The fire of the altar was to be kept burning. There were the morning and the evening burnt offerings. The sweet fragrance of the morning sacrifice had not died away till the evening fragrance began to ascend. Thus God had the constant delight of feeding on the sweet incense cloud that went up from the copper altar. It was the sweet savour of Christ. In His life this caused God at the commencement of the Lord's public path to exclaim, "This is My beloved Son, in whom I am well pleased." It was this that occasioned the voice out of heaven, near the time of the cross, "I have both glorified it (His name), and will glorify it again" (John 12:28). The life and death of the Lord Jesus was one continuous ascending offering - the fragrance of His life, and the fragrance of His death. There would appear to be a connection between the morning and evening sacrifice and the fact that the Lord was crucified at the third hour, and died at the ninth hour of the day.

Lastly, we note that God had a care for the ashes of the burnt offering. The priest with appropriate garments had to take up the ashes from the hearth of the altar, place them on the east side of the altar, change his garments, and carry forth the ashes to a clean place without the camp. Here in shadow we trace Nicodemus with Joseph doing that great work of taking down the precious body of the Lord Jesus, and carrying it when anointed and wrapped in the new linen clothes to a clean place - a new tomb, wherein was never man yet laid. Thus morning by morning during the desert journey God saw in shadow what was to be done to His Son. There was a daily rehearsal in shadow of that great event. Glad in heart are we that that tomb could not retain God's Son. The third morning He arose in the power of an endless life. Now He is on the throne above, and continues to delight the heart of His God.

"Thou God of glorious majesty,

What can we render unto Thee

For all that Thou for us hast done

In Christ Thy well-beloved Son?

When Israel's sons Thy presence sought,

Acceptably to Thee they brought,

As meet thank-offerings to be,

The best of that received from Thee.

As reverently Thy courts they trod

They praised and worshipped Thee their God,

For victories Thine arm achieved,

For earthly benefits received.

Then what more fitting now can we,

Give, O Thou Blessed God, to Thee

Than of the best that Thou hast given

Thy gift of gifts sent down from heaven?"

CHAPTER TWO: THE MEAL OFFERING

The meal offering of Leviticus 2 presents a type of our Lord Jesus Christ as the perfect Man. As there is no blood-shedding in this oblation it sets forth the Man Christ Jesus in His life, whereas the burnt offering with which we dealt in the previous chapter sets Him forth in His death upon the cross of Calvary. The true humanity of the Lord Jesus is a subject that is dear to the hearts of all who have come to know Him; and there can be no greater delight to the godly soul than that of musing upon the perfections of Christ as revealed in the sacred, holy Scriptures of truth.

The great enemy of souls has been successful in deluding myriads in respect to who Christ is, the real nature of His Person, and the manner designed by God for His entrance as a Man into this world. Modernism has a Christ who is similar to that conceived by men at the close of the first century, and which denies the truth of the virgin birth of our Lord. Unwilling to admit the miraculous in the birth of Christ, they teach that He was the natural son of Joseph and Mary, though they fail to recognize that this involves just as great a miracle, that of a sinless Offspring from sinful parents; the Divine from the purely human. This would involve interference with the physical and psychical order of the universe.

We can turn to the Scriptures and there find the breathings of God's Holy Spirit upon this important subject, and be assured that we are at the fountain-head of truth, in the region of divine revelation. But how fitting for us to approach with unshod feet, for the ground we shall tread is holy! Here we may discern the Shepherd's voice, since we have come to know Him, and by listening to Him we will flee from the voice of strangers.

Of the meal offering, then, we read, "His oblation shall be of fine flour; and he shall pour oil upon it, and put frankincense thereon." This fine flour typifies Christ in the evenness of His character, in His yieldingness in the hand of His God, and in His gentle ways as He moved amidst our ruined race. He was perfect in word and in deed. Of Him it has been said that "every moral quality met in divine, and therefore, perfect proportion. No one feature preponderated." This is true indeed. The Canaanite woman had no claim upon Him as Son of David, so He answers her not a word. Barren of sympathy the disciples say, Send her away; for she crieth after us." But when she approached as a humble suppliant, taking the place of a Gentile dog, He said, "O woman, great is thy faith: be it done unto thee even as thou wilt." He was particular as to what claim was made upon Him, and the woman had no such claim as her first words of address implied; but how gladly He allowed His mercy and power to flow when the proper position was taken! "And her daughter was healed from that hour" (Matthew 15:21-28). Mercy had found the proper channel.

The Lord Jesus says of Himself, "I am meek (Greek, 'praos': meek, mild, soft) and lowly in heart." He was like the fine flour in the hand of God, soft, yielding, impressible. Never did He resist the Holy Spirit. He was in this unlike the Israel people of whom Stephen said, "Ye do always resist the Holy Spirit: as your fathers did, so do ye." If the Spirit led to the wilderness to those trying days of hunger and temptation, He was ready and willing to respond. If the leading was to Jerusalem where trial and death were awaiting Him, He could say to the Pharisees, "I must go on my way today and tomorrow and the day following: for it cannot be that a prophet perish out of Jerusalem." Even to Peter's outburst, "Be it far from Thee, Lord: this shall never be unto Thee," He replied, "Get thee behind Me, Satan: thou art a stumbling-block unto Me: for thou mindest not the things of God, but the things of men."

Amazingly balanced were the human and the Divine. View Him arising from sleep to quell the storm and sea. Weakness was enjoying refreshment in sleep, Omnipotence commanded the wind and the deep.

"Calm and majestic rises from His pillow

Sea's mighty Lord, commanding, Peace, be still

Sink then to rest, with troubled wind and billow,

Their tossing minds, soothed by His potent will."

Pity and power blended with divine perfection whilst He moved among the sorrowing. As He met the funeral procession near the city of Nain there was a pity that wiped the widow's tear; and a power that quickened her son on the bier. His own tears flowed near Lazarus' grave, whom He called to life through His power to save. Generosity and frugality were evidenced in His feeding of the multitudes. "They have no need to go away; give ye them to eat ... and they all did eat, and were filled." Here His munificence shines. Then He commands, "Gather up the broken pieces which remain over, that nothing be lost." In this we see economy. With Him there was not anything stingy on the one hand, or extravagant or wasteful on the other hand. In His prostration and supplication in the garden of Gethsemane we behold the humble Man: in His words to the traitor-band we hear the great I AM. Self-prostration and self-possession are shown forth. Before enemies there was a power to overawe; for the needy there was a kindliness to draw.

"Wist ye not that I must be in the things of My Father?" is in agreement with the attitude of the Nazirite (see Numbers 6). The true Nazirite said to His mother, "Woman, what have I to do with thee?" The Son with the perfect human heart said to John the beloved disciple, "Behold thy mother." "And He went down with them, and came to Nazareth; and He was subject unto them," is in keeping with, "Ye shall fear every man his mother, and his father" (Leviticus 19:3). All through His life we see the perfection of the fine flour, that evenness, yieldingness, softness in the hand of God's Spirit; every act and word being the result of the Spirit's movement within Him. With the woman in the Song of Songs we can say, "Yea, He is altogether lovely. This is my Beloved, and this is my Friend."

Besides the fine flour in the meal offering there was oil. The oil is a type of the blessed Holy Spirit, and we should note three things that are mentioned in connection with the oil; the flour or cakes had oil mingled; the unleavened wafers were anointed with oil; and there were cakes of fine flour soaked with oil.

That flour and those unleavened cakes mingled with oil, cause us to think of the conception of the Lord Jesus by the Holy Spirit. In Hebrews 10:5 we read, "When He cometh into the world, He saith, Sacrifice and offering Thou wouldest not, But a body didst Thou prepare for Me." Isaiah had foretold that "A virgin shall conceive, and bear a Son, and shall call His name Immanuel" (Isaiah 7:14), and in the Gospel by Luke we have recorded some of the most precious revealings, set forth with a sensitiveness wholly in keeping with the subject. Mary was that virgin. To her, Gabriel said, "Thou shalt conceive in thy womb, and bring forth a Son, and shalt call His name JESUS ... The Holy Spirit shall come upon thee, and the power of the Most High shall overshadow thee: wherefore also the Holy Thing which is to be born shall be called the Son of God" (Luke 1:31,85, RV margin).

Here we have the truth concerning the humanity of Christ, a humanity that was without a taint of sin. Blessed be God for preparing such a body for His Son; and blessed be the Son of God who came as it is written in the roll of the book, "To do Thy will,

O God"! (Hebrews 10:7). From all eternity He had been in the bosom of the Father; but now God, in the fulness of the time, hath "sent forth His Son, born of a woman, born under the law" (Galatians 4:4). Here is One who is God and Man in one combined, a glorious, unique Person, like whom there is not another in all the universe of God. Happy are all who, like Thomas, can say, My Lord and my God." He is "Christ who is over all, God blessed for ever. Amen" (Romans 9:5).

In the unleavened cakes anointed with oil, we are caused to consider Him who when He was setting out on His public ministry was anointed by the Holy Spirit. "Jesus also having been baptized, and praying, the heaven was opened, and the Holy Spirit descended in a bodily form, as a dove, upon Him, and a voice came out of heaven, Thou art My beloved Son; in Thee I am well pleased" (Luke 3:21-22). Then as we think of the fine flour soaked with oil we recall the verse, "And Jesus, full of the Holy Spirit, returned from the Jordan, and was led by the Spirit in the wilderness." All He did was by the Spirit's power. Though Himself the very Son of God, yet it was by the Spirit of God He cast out demons, and performed His many works, which delighted His Father in heaven, and brought such unspeakable blessing to men. Peter told "How that God anointed Him with the Holy Spirit and with power: who went about doing good, and healing all that were oppressed of the devil; for God was with Him" (Acts 10:38).

We have now to consider the frankincense and the salt which were ingredients in the meal offering. The frankincense was put upon the flour and the oil, and in the memorial which was burned on the altar all the frankincense was taken and went up to God in a sweet savour. This shows that it speaks of that in the life of the Lord Jesus which was all for God. The priests could partake of the flour and oil, but not of the frankincense. While there is so much for us in the lovely life of Christ, we recognize there was that which was all for the glory of His God. Vast and continuous was that fragrance that went up to God from His Son-from His thoughts, His words, His deeds. True are those words of His in John 17. "I glorified Thee upon the earth, having accomplished the work which Thou gavest Me to do." The fire of the altar brought out the sweet fragrance of the frankincense, and the trials of the Lord Jesus only brought out the sweetness of His Person and work. As He did the will of God amid constant opposition the heart of God was refreshed by the frankincense, an odour of a sweet smell.

Salt had to be in all the oblations - the salt of the covenant. We know that salt is a preservative, it checks and stops corruption. The Spirit associates the seasoning with salt, with speech, as in Colossians 4:6; and we recall how in the speakings of the Lord Jesus there was so frequently the evidence of the salt. His words were not without their effect on the corrupt thoughts and ways of those around Him. The salt was not lacking

Honey and leaven were to be omitted from the meal offering. Honey might remind us of the natural sweetness which is not desired by God; and leaven usually speaks of evil, of malice and wickedness. Nothing of these was in the Lord Jesus. Then there were three forms in which the meal offering could be offered: cakes baked in the oven; cakes baked on a flat plate or frying pan; bruised corn parched before the fire. These speak to us of varying degrees of suffering or trial: in the oven, the greatest, since the heat was from every side: the flat plate or frying pan, the lesser, since the heat was from beneath; before the fire, the least, in the case of the parched corn. Possibly this least is suggestive of His sufferings from the hands of Man; that from beneath, as His sufferings from the hands of the hosts of the underworld, with Satan at their head: the greatest trials were those endured as under the hand of God. That He did suffer thus we are fully assured.

"For ever on Thy burdened heart

A weight of sorrow hung;

Yet no ungentle, murmuring word

Escaped Thy silent tongue."

CHAPTER THREE: THE PEACE OFFERING

Fellowship is a predominant feature in the peace offering. Like the burnt offering it typifies Christ in His death; but unlike the burnt offering which was all for God there is in the peace offering, as shadowing the Person and work of the Lord Jesus, a portion for God, a portion for the priests, and a portion for the worshippers who brought the oblation.

John's first epistle opens with this precious theme - fellowship. Referring to the Word of Life which was from the beginning, John writes, "And the Life was manifested, and we have seen, and bear witness, and declare unto you the life, the eternal life, which was with the Father, and was manifested unto us); that which we have seen and heard declare we unto you also, that ye also may have fellowship with us: yea, and our fellowship is with the Father, and with His Son Jesus Christ: and these things we write, that our joy may be fulfilled" (1 John 1:2-4).

It should be observed that there could be no communion or fellowship with God on the part of sin-stained humanity apart from the death of Christ. This verse 7 of 1 John 1 makes clear and plain, where we read, "If we walk in the light, as He is in the light, we have fellowship one with another, and the blood of Jesus His Son cleanseth us from all sin." The cleansing of the blood is necessary, since God cannot have contact with that which is unclean. He is Light, and His light cannot have communion with our darkness. Experiencing the cleansing of the blood we are brought into the light of God's presence, and there our fellowship is real one with another, and with the Father, and with His Son Jesus Christ. Happy portion indeed! Thus and thus only can full Christian joy be known.

The story of the prodigal who returned to his father from the darkness and dearth of the far-off land is full of precious teaching in this respect. At that feast around the fatted calf where joy abounded, and particularly so for the father, the young man had been cleansed and clothed for the occasion. There could have been no joy for any concerned had he not parted from the evidence and results of his prodigality. But be it noted, all was provided for him by a forgiving father.

So it is with us who call on God as Father, He has provided everything we require for our entrance into this condition of happiness; and in the peace offering we may learn much as to His liberal provision. He is still Jehovah-jireh, the great Provider.

Coming now to Leviticus 3, we find the peace offering could be from herd or flock, but there is no mention of an oblation of peace offerings from the birds. This would surely indicate that some measure of spiritual attainment is expected where true fellowship is known, since the birds suggest the lowest measure of spiritual perception of the trio indicated in Leviticus 1. There is a prohibition, however, which calls for comment, namely, "It shall be a perpetual statute throughout your generations in all your dwellings, that ye shall eat neither fat nor blood" (verse 17). Since abstinence from blood was in the prohibitions sent out to the churches of God in the early days of the apostles, it follows that it is enjoined on us who are in the Fellowship of God's Son today. There is no restriction in regard to the fat, but with us blood should be eschewed.

We have already mentioned that in the peace offering there is a portion for God, for the priests, and for the worshippers; but let us consider for a moment that in chapter 3 of Leviticus there is no mention of anything for priests and people - it is only God's portion that is here before us. In the law of the peace offering in chapter 7 we find man's share, and a liberal part or portion it is, but Leviticus 3 indicates that God must be first. This is characteristic and fundamental, God must be first; He will not, indeed cannot because of His Being, be relegated to a second place. Those who put themselves first, must encounter judgement. Of such are the sons of Eli, the priest. Of these we read: "When any man offered sacrifice (peace offerings, I judge), the priest's servant came, while the flesh was in seething, with a fleshhook of three teeth in his hand; and he struck it into the pan, or kettle, or caldron, or pot; all that the fleshhook brought up the priest took therewith ... Yea, before they burnt the fat, the priest's servant came, and said ... Give flesh to roast for the priest ... and the sin of the young men was very great" (1 Samuel 2:18-17). These two young men, the priests, died by the sword very shortly afterwards.

A further contrast with the burnt offering is seen in that the peace offering could be either male or female. The burnt offering had to be a male only. The male represented the highest in value in the type, and as the burnt offering set forth Christ as offering up Himself to God, and all for God, it shows that God's valuation of His Son was of the very highest. In the peace offering, however, where there is a portion for man, he could bring either male or female.

God's portion, then, was the best of the animals. "The fat that covereth the inwards, and all the fat that is upon the inwards, and the two kidneys, and the fat that is on them, which is by the loins, and the caul upon the liver, with the kidneys, shall he take away. And Aaron's sons shall burn it on the altar upon the burnt offering, which is upon the wood that is on the fire: it is an offering made by fire, of a sweet savour unto the LORD" (Leviticus 3:3-5). "It is the food of the offering made by fire unto the LORD" (verse 11). Yes, God's food was on that altar, the best of the victim, and the whole spoke of Christ. It was a sweet savour of Christ unto God.

Before we leave chapter 3 we must draw attention to verse 2: "And he shall lay his hand upon the head of his oblation, and kill it at the door of the tent of meeting: and Aaron's sons the priests shall sprinkle the blood upon the altar round about." Here we find the offerer being identified with the victim as he lays his hand upon its head. We have been identified with Christ through our faith in Him. The door of the tent of meeting reminds us of the one Place which is so emphasized in Holy Scripture. The sprinkling of the blood round the altar, where the eyes of the offerer could gaze upon it, would speak of that which is the base of all communion with God - the shed and sprinkled blood, even the blood of Christ, who has "made peace through the blood pf His cross" (Colossians 1:20). "Ye that once were afar off are made nigh in the blood of Christ. For He is our peace" (Ephesians 2:13,14). Micah 5:5 is true, "This Man shall be our peace." Every claim of divine holiness has been met by that precious blood, and in consequence the believer in Christ can rest in absolute confidence before God. It is thus that fellowship with God is secured. There are no other means possible.

We come now to the portion that was given to the priests. "The priest shall burn the fat upon the altar: but the breast shall be Aaron's and his sons'. And the right thigh (shoulder) shall ye give unto the priest for an heave offering out of the sacrifices of your peace offerings. He among the sons of Aaron, that offereth the blood of the peace offerings, and the fat, shall have the right thigh (shoulder) for a portion. For the wave breast and the heave thigh (shoulder) have I taken of the children of Israel out of the sacrifices of their peace offerings, and have given them unto Aaron the priest and unto his sons as a due for ever from the children of Israel" (Leviticus 7:31-34).

The breast and the shoulder take our thoughts to the Lord Jesus. We think of His shoulders, and of the place we have there. It is the place of omnipotent strength. Here is something to feast upon indeed. It is the place on which the Shepherd puts His sheep when He finds it. Thence He is responsible to take it home. "He will not fail, He cannot faint, Salvation's sure, and must be mine."

Those stones on the high priest's shoulders remind us of the security of the believer, since on them were engraven the names of the children of Israel, according to their birth. What a joy it is to be fully assured that our names are on the shoulders of our High Priest, there for a memorial in the immediate presence of God! We think of the words of the Lord to the disciples, "Rejoice that your names are written in heaven" (Luke 10:20). Nothing on earth is comparable to this. Earthly honours and memorials will pass away and perish for ever, but here is something which is abiding. Think of the bliss of having in present possession the gift of eternal life, and to know that we shall never perish! This is what our Shepherd assures us of. Let us, like the priests of old who fed upon the shoulder, feed upon our blessed portion in Christ!

There is a beauty about the fact that "he among the sons of Aaron, that offereth the blood of the peace offerings, and the fat, shall have the right shoulder for a portion" (verse 83). It would seem to tell us that occupation with the blood, and what it means to us, and being taken up with that which is God's portion in His Son, is in agreement with enjoyment of the precious truths suggested by the shoulders. One thing is certain, if we fail to discern the value of the blood, and the delight which God finds in the work of His Son, a work that has given Him infinite satisfaction, we are unlikely to set the true value on His work that has secured eternal salvation for us.

Coming now to the breast of the peace offering we think of the breast of our great Sacrifice. If the shoulder is the place of strength, the breast is the place of love and affection. What a place for us to have access to! What wonderful love and affection are His! Indeed it is in the measure that we are enjoying fellowship with God that we will know what this affection is experimentally. How much do we know of what is said in Song of Songs 1:2,4? "Let Him kiss me with the kisses of His mouth, for Thy love is better than wine and, the king hath brought me into His chamber: We will be glad and rejoice in Thee, We will make mention of Thy love more than of wine: Rightly do they love Thee."

Wine maketh glad the heart of man, and Jotham the son of Jerubbaal said, or caused the vine to say, "Should I leave my vine, which cheereth God and man?" Yes, wine is the symbol of that which maketh man glad naturally, but here is something that is better than wine-Thy love is better than wine. As Aaron and his sons fed on the breast, let us also feed on the affections of the everlasting Lover of our unworthy race. He says, "Even as the Father hath loved Me, I also have loved you: abide ye in My love" (John 15:9). And let us keep well in mind that Himself has said, "If a man love Me, he will keep My word: and My Father will love him, and we will come unto him, and make Our abode with him" (John 14:23). This is fellowship indeed.

"He loves us deeply, this we know

By tokens that He wears;

Pierced hands, and feet, and side, all show

The matchless love He bears."

Then what was the portion of the worshipper in the peace offering? Take away the fat, take away the breast and shoulder, then all that is left of the animal was for the worshippers to feast upon. It was a large portion. As we see these sit down to feast, we have complete the picture of fellowship - God has His portion from the altar, the priests have theirs in the breast and shoulder, and the worshippers have theirs in the remainder of the sacrifice. Thank God all this speaks of the vast provision there is in Christ our great Peace Offering. Oh to know more of feeding upon Him - feeding in happy fellowship with God, for truly our fellowship is with the Father, and with His Son Jesus Christ."

The condition of those who partook of the peace offerings calls for earnest attention. God said, "As for the flesh, every one that is clean shall eat thereof: but the soul that eateth of the flesh of the sacrifice of peace offerings, that pertain unto the LORD, having his uncleanness upon him, that soul shall be cut off from his people" (Leviticus 7:19,20). How close is the agreement between the shadows of the Old Covenant and the substance of the New Covenant! The Holy Spirit who arranged the shadows has also given us the substance. So He tells us through John: "This is the message which we have heard from Him, and announce unto you, that God is light, and in Him is no darkness at all. If we say that we have fellowship with Him, and walk in the darkness, we lie, and do not the truth: but if we walk in the light, as He is in the light, we have fellowship one with another, and the blood of Jesus His Son cleanseth us from all sin" (1 John 1:5-7).

How careful we need to be that we do not have unconfessed sin upon us! It is this that brings the darkness of which John writes. Sin acts like a thick cloud between God and us. Confession on our part, and the blood on the part of Christ, are the means for the dispersal of the dark cloud, and the securing of fellowship with God and His Son.

Perhaps it is this failure in confession, and lack of laying hold upon the value of Christ's atonement through His death, that is the cause of the many dwarfs among the children of God. To grow spiritually we must feed upon Christ, feed upon Him in fellowship with God; but if we continue in uncleanness we are not able to feed and grow. We become stinted in growth, and feeble in strength. Let us, though having sin in us, our fallen nature, see to it that sin is not upon us, shutting out the light of the divine presence! It has been said truly, "It is good to keep short accounts with God." Let us be frank in our approach to and confessions before God, remembering that He knows all and He will assist us in this. We may hide faults from one another, but nothing is hid from Him, "and there is no creature that is not manifest in His sight: but all things are naked and laid open before the eyes of Him with whom we have to do" (Hebrews 4:18).

CHAPTER FOUR: THE SIN OFFERING

Bible reading: Leviticus 4:1-5,18.

We now come to a class of offerings distinct from those sweet savour offerings in chapters 1 to 3. In the sin offerings, sin had to be dealt with in such a manner that Jehovah in His holiness and righteousness might be satisfied. This is a matter of immense importance since the manner of dealing with sin must be according to the divine estimate, and not merely what man might judge necessary. The sinner must listen to God's requirements and act accordingly if he is to know acceptance.

In this offering the first thing mentioned by the LORD is the nature of the sin – "If any one shall sin unwittingly." We discern at once that the LORD is not making provision in connection with presumptuous sin, which is of an entirely different nature. "When ye shall err," says the LORD, "and not observe all these commandments which the LORD hath spoken unto Moses ... then it shall be ... if one person sins unwittingly, then he shall offer ... a sin offering to make atonement for him, and he shall be forgiven ... But the soul that doeth aught with an high hand, whether he be homeborn or a stranger, the same blasphemeth the LORD; and that soul shall be cut off from among his people. Because he hath despised the word of the LORD, and hath broken His commandment; that soul shall be utterly cut off, his iniquity shall be upon him" (Numbers 15:22-31).

A striking example of one whose iniquity was upon him on account of presumptuous sin is Joab, the captain of David's host. As he clung to the altar hoping to escape from judgement,

Solomon commanded, "Fall upon him, and bury him ... And the LORD shall return his blood upon his own head, because he fell upon two men more righteous and better than he, and slew them with the sword ... to wit, Abner the son of Ner, captain of the host of Israel, and Amasa the son of Jether, captain of the host of Judah. So shall their blood return upon the head of Joab, and upon the head of his seed for ever" (1 Kings 2:5,6,31-33). For one who found no place of repentance the altar could afford no protection. This is a solemn reminder that Calvary with its wondrous Victim and its flood-tide of mercy for the guilty is no place for unrepentant sinners. "Repentance toward God, and faith toward our Lord Jesus Christ" (Acts 20:21) must ever be essentials in obtaining forgiveness and salvation; and we who belong to Christ may well pray as David prayed, in Psalm 19:18.

In Leviticus 4:8 are two Hebrew words, 'chata', to miss the mark, to wander from the way, or, to stumble in the path of rectitude; and 'ashmah', to become guilty, to trespass: "If the anointed priest shall sin (chata) so as to bring guilt (ashmah) on the people: then let him offer for his sin, which he hath sinned, a young bullock without blemish unto the LORD for a sin offering." Sin brings guilt, and it is good when we become conscious of the guilt incurred. Too often, alas, the consciousness of guilt is lacking where there is a missing of the mark, a stumbling in the path of rectitude.

But where the conscience is awakened there is the longing for clearance from guilt, and it is here that the LORD made gracious provision. So also in writing to Timothy Paul refers to certain things which had caused persons to err concerning the faith, or miss the mark. Among these are "the profane babblings and oppositions of the knowledge which is falsely so called" (6:20); "the love of money ... a root of all kinds of evil" (6:10); "to be idle" (5:18); and "giving heed to seducing spirits and doctrines of demons" (4:1). How needful in these deceptive days that we take heed that no one leads us astray! But if in anything we miss the mark and be guilty let us seek unto God and the provision He has made.

There was a wide range in the sin offering. It started with the bullock in the case of an anointed priest, or the whole congregation, then a male of the goats for a ruler, a female of the goats for one of the common people, and for one who was poor resort could be had to two birds, whilst for one extremely poor the tenth part of an ephah of fine flour without oil or frankincense could be brought, a handful of which as a memorial thereof was burnt on the altar, upon the offering of the LORD made by fire. And whether it was the bullock offering with its high value or the handful of fine flour it is delightful to read the assuring words, "and he shall be forgiven." Did the writer to the Hebrews have this handful of fine flour in mind when he wrote, "And according to the law, I may almost say, all things are cleansed with blood"? (Hebrews 9:22). It appears to me that he had. How sweet is the fact of the forgiveness of sins! Some of us have a special place in our hearts for the message of Acts 10:48, "To Him (Christ) bear all the prophets witness, that through His name every one that believeth on Him shall receive remission of sins."

The law of the sin offering states, "it is most holy," and it is worthy of careful attention that the Spirit of God asserts this in this class of offering. Seeing it was made an offering for sin and took the sinner's place beneath the judgement of God we might have been inclined to the thought that it was the opposite of most holy, or "holy of holies"; but no, God's word is plain and definite. "And whatsoever shall touch the flesh thereof," saith the LORD, "shall be holy." From this we may learn much concerning the blessed Lord Jesus when as the Sin-bearer He occupied the cruel cross for us. Even there while He bore the curse He was still holy before God. Blessed adorable Saviour! How our hearts should go out to Him for the grace that enabled Him to taste death for sinners.

The offerer laid his hand upon the head of the victim, thus identifying himself with the offering, and thereby acknowledging that it was to take his place in death. The animal was slain and the blood applied as the LORD directed. Much may be learned from the sprinkling of the blood. In the case of the anointed priest or the congregation the blood was taken into the holy place and sprinkled seven times before the veil of the sanctuary. Why, we may ask? Surely it was because of the far-reaching effects of sin. The sanctuary was God's dwelling place, and sin in the camp would have driven God from His resting place over the mercy-seat unless it was atoned for by the sprinkled blood. What a dreadful thing sin is! It brought about the condition described in Lamentations 2:6-7, "He hath violently taken away His tabernacle, as if it were a garden; He hath destroyed His place of assembly: the LORD hath caused solemn assembly and sabbath to be forgotten in Zion ... The Lord hath cast off His altar, He hath abhorred His Sanctuary." While men of the world think lightly of sin, some even denying that it exists at all, believers in the Lord Jesus should be alert to its enormity, and should learn to hate it as God does.

Next the blood was put on the horns of the altar of sweet incense. Again we ask, why? and here we should consider that this altar was the place from which went up to God the sweet savour of the incense that was compounded from the stacte and onycha and galbanum, sweet spices with pure frankincense - all suggestive of the sweet fragrance of Christ in the heavenly sanctuary. The prayers and worship of the people went up to God with this sweet fragrance from the incense altar (Revelation 8:8).

The blood applied to the horns of this altar reminds us that sin would affect this also. Unless it be atoned for, sin would rob God of His portion from His people, but the blood applied to the horns of the altar made atonement and secured that holiness that becomes God's dwelling place. There is yet another place where the blood is seen, this is at the copper altar at the door of the house. "All the blood of the bullock shall he pour out at the base of the altar of burnt offering." Thus atonement was made for the sinner. As the people saw that crimson flow they had joy and the satisfaction of knowing atonement for them was complete. Sin had been dealt with as a holy God required, and fellowship with Him was restored. We, too, gladly sing those well-known words of the hymn: "His blood can make the foulest clean, His blood avails for me," and we bless God for "a merciful and faithful High Priest in things pertaining to God, to make propitiation for the sins of the people" (Hebrews 2:17), even our Lord Jesus Christ.

It is well to keep before us the different aspects of the death of Christ seen in the sin offering. John the Baptist cried, "Behold, the Lamb of God, which taketh away the sin of the world" (John 1:29), this was something wider and greater than is found in the type, and in his first epistle John the son of Zebedee says, "He is the propitiation for our sins; and not for ours only, but also for the whole world" (2:2). This is in keeping with "Christ Jesus who gave Himself a Ransom for all" (1 Timothy 2:5,6); but it is the blood of the sin offering for the congregation that is contemplated in Hebrews 13:11,12, where we read, "For the bodies of those beasts whose blood is brought into the holy place by the high priest as an offering for sin, are burnt without the camp. Wherefore Jesus also, that He might sanctify the people through His own blood, suffered without the gate."

As we have seen in the case of an individual, such as a ruler or one of the common people the blood was applied to the copper altar only, it was not taken inside the holy place, but the Lord Jesus had the sanctification of the people in view (a collective people) and therefore He suffered without the gate, and then "through His own blood, entered in once for all into the holy place, having obtained eternal redemption" (Hebrews 9:12).

But more than that, it calls to us from the sanctuary above to "go forth unto Him without the camp, bearing His reproach." We should not dread the place of rejection with Him. Let us consider that He took the lonely outside place for us, and that He suffered more than tongue can tell. This was because of His love for us. Let us show our love to Him by our obedience to this call to go forth unto Him without the camp, bearing His reproach.

God's portion of the sin offering was the fat, the two kidneys, and the caul upon the liver; these were placed on the altar of burnt offering and ascended as a sweet savour to God. Referring to the priests God said, "They shall be holy unto their God ... for the offerings of the LORD made by fire, the bread of their God, they do offer." Thus what went up from the altar, and what the priests ate was the bread or food of God (Leviticus 21:6,22). But if the blood was taken within the holy place the priests did not eat of the flesh; the whole animal "shall he carry forth without the camp unto a clean place, where the ashes are poured out, and burn it on wood with fire" (Leviticus 4:12).

"Burn" here is from the Hebrew word 'saraph', to burn up, and the notion we should gather may be found in some of the uses of the word by the Spirit of God, as for instance, "that which remaineth of it (the passover) until the morning ye shall burn with fire" (Exodus 12:10); "The graven images of their gods shall ye burn with fire" (Deuteronomy 7:25); "And they burnt the city with fire" (Joshua 6:24). Obviously judgement is indicated, and the shadow takes our minds to the Saviour's lonely sufferings beneath the judgement hand of God when He bore the stroke which was due to us, and we hear His orphan cry, "My God, My God, why hast Thou forsaken Me?" We hear the answer also in the prophetic words, "But Thou art holy, O Thou that inhabitest the praises of Israel" (Psalm 22:3).

The word 'qatar' is used for that burnt on the altar, and the thought seems to be that as of burning incense, something that was sweet and precious to God. Precious mysteries of the cross are thus presented to us, for there He bore our judgement, and also there He gave to God that which delighted the heart of God - the food or bread of God.

"If his means suffice not for a lamb, then he shall bring for his guilt for that wherein he hath sinned, two turtledoves, or two young pigeons" (5:7, RV margin). It is touching to recall that He of whom it is written, "Praise Him for His mighty acts, Praise Him according to His excellent greatness (Psalm 150:2), should stoop down to sojourn in the home of parents whose means sufficed not for a lamb, for ... "they brought Him to Jerusalem, to present Him to the Lord ... and to offer a sacrifice ... a pair of turtledoves, or two young pigeons" (Luke 2:22-24). As He grew up and moved among men He had not where to lay His head, and at the cross He knew the experience foretold by Daniel the prophet, "And after threescore and two weeks shall the Anointed One be cut off, and shall have nothing" (9:26). Thank God for His Son, "who loved me, and gave Himself up for me." "Him who knew no sin He made to be sin (sin-offering) on our behalf; that we might become the righteousness of God in Him."

"Crowned with thorns upon the tree,

Silent in His agony

Dying crushed beneath the load

Of the wrath and curse of God.

On his pale and suffering brow,

Mystery of love and woe;

On His grief and sore amaze

We would fix our earnest gaze.

Sin-atoning sacrifice,

Oh how precious in our eyes!

He alone our rest shall be,

Now and through eternity."

CHAPTER FIVE: THE GUILT OFFERING

In the Guilt or Trespass offering the Lord required a ram without blemish, according to the priest's estimation in silver by shekels, after the shekel of the sanctuary (Leviticus 5:15). Here a contrast is seen as against the sin offering which, as we have shown, could be a bullock, a ram, a lamb, or birds, or even fine flour. The shekel of the sanctuary reminds us that the evaluation of the sacrifice must be after God's standard, and not according to that of the one who commits the trespass.

There are many who regard their own doings as sufficient to satisfy God in respect to their guilt: but no! The guilty one must listen to what God requires, and accept God's conditions and remedy. It was just here that Cain went wrong. Both Abel and he desired to be accepted by God, hence their offerings; but instead of attending to what a thrice-holy God required he brought what he had produced from his tilling of the ground, only to find that he was rejected. Alas! that there are so many like Cain today who vainly hope for acceptance with God on the ground of their good works, though God has spoken so plainly in the matter, as in the words, "All our righteousnesses are as a polluted garment" (Isaiah 64:6).

The trespass and guilt of man brought death, and in the epistle to the Romans, which presents the doctrine of the gospel, we find the divine evaluation for the Trespass Offering - One who is the Son of God, Jesus Christ our Lord (Romans 1:3,4). He is of such infinite worth that only God Himself can estimate His value. Adam, who trespassed, is a figure of Him that was to come, and by the trespass of the one the many died, and death reigned, and the judgement came unto all men to condemnation; but through Him who became the great Trespass Offering the grace of God, and the gift by the grace of the one Man, Jesus Christ, abound unto the many (see Romans 5:12-21). He "was delivered up for our trespasses, and was raised for our justification" (4:25).

With David we can say, "Blessed is he whose transgression is forgiven, whose sin is covered. Blessed is the man unto whom the LORD imputeth not iniquity" (Psalm 32:1-2).

Sin has been spoken of as the root, transgression as the shoot, and iniquity as the fruit. There is in our nature a root of sin as the result of the Fall, and from it spring the trespasses, the transgressions, which are hateful to God, and harmful to men; and both sin and trespass offerings of Leviticus 4, 5 and 6 have to do with sins and trespasses which spring from that root of sin within. How pleasing for us to appreciate that the cross-work of Christ has dealt with sin as to root, shoot and fruit! There is therefore in the Person and work of the Lord Jesus provision for our every need. "The free gift came of many trespasses unto justification," and thereafter we can come and claim the value of the blood for sins and trespasses which we confess and know will be forgiven, because He, Jesus Christ our Advocate, "is the propitiation for our sins" (1 John 2:1-2).

Of the trespass offering then we read, "If any one commit a trespass, and sin unwittingly, in the holy things of the LORD; then he shall bring ... a ram without blemish" (Leviticus 5: 15). These holy things would include things set apart for the LORD, as the firstlings of flock or herd. These the LORD claimed. "The firstling of an ox, or the firstling of a sheep, or the firstling of a goat, thou shalt not redeem; they are holy: thou shalt sprinkle their blood upon the altar, and shalt burn their fat for an offering made by fire, for a sweet savour unto the LORD. And the flesh of them shall be thine, as the wave breast and as the right thigh, it shall be thine. All the heave offerings of the holy things, which the children of Israel offer unto the LORD, have I given thee" (Numbers 18:17-19). It was truly possible for an Israelite or a priest to trespass in these holy things of the LORD. Then the one who had erred "shall bring his guilt offering unto the LORD, a ram without blemish."

Like the other offerings it had to be perfect to be accepted, and thus it was a type of Christ, the perfect One of whom it is written, "Thou shalt make His soul a guilt offering" (Isaiah 53:10 RV margin). This perfection on the part of Christ is indicated in the words, "Jesus Christ the righteous ... the propitiation for our sins." He was righteousness personified.

Not alone did the LORD require a ram to be offered where there was a trespass in the holy things, but He also ordered that restitution be made, and this with the fifth part added was to be given to the priest. Thus there was the ram for a sacrifice, the value of the thing in question restored, and the fifth part of the value added. This matter of restitution is a feature in the trespass offering. It is not seen in the other offerings. What comfort to us to realize that He who is our Trespass Offering has made the restitution shadowed here! Of Him it is prophetically written, "Then I restored that which I took not away" (Psalm 69:4). All that was lost to God in the Fall has been restored to God by our great Trespass Offering, but more than that, He has added to it. In truth it has been said that God gains more in redemption than He lost in the Fall. There will be a richer harvest from the fields of redemption than could have come from creation: there will be a more lofty song, in view of the empty tomb, than from the wonders of creation. Wrong has not only been righted, but an eternal advantage gained by the work of the cross.

We have now to draw attention to the closing paragraph of Leviticus 5. "If any one sin, and do any of the things which the LORD hath commanded not to be done; though he knew it not, yet is he guilty, and shall bear his iniquity" (verse 17). Lack of knowledge does not exonerate. It is also so in the law of England. It is futile to plead ignorance when we break the law, and so with the law of the LORD, "though he knew it not, yet is he guilty." This should cause us to be diligent to know and understand the will of the Lord, and give effect to it, for God will hold us responsible seeing He has caused His will to be made known in the Holy Scriptures. The trespass or guilt offering had to be brought when the trespass was discovered, and the assurance is given that "he shall be forgiven." There are sins of omission as well as commission, and we wonder that so many of the Lord's dear children are without concern in respect to such commands as disciples' baptism, and "this do in remembrance of Me." Oh that such persons would "cease to do evil," and, "learn to do well"! Then forgiveness could be theirs also.

There were two classes of trespass offerings, (1) that in the holy things, and (2) trespass against a neighbour. In the former the order is sacrifice and restitution; in the second it is restitution and sacrifice. "Then it shall be, if he hath sinned, and is guilty, that he shall restore that which he took by robbery, or the thing which he hath gotten by oppression, or the deposit which was committed to him, or the lost thing which he found, or any thing about which he hath sworn falsely; he shall even restore it in full, and shall add the fifth part more thereto: unto him to whom it appertaineth shall he give it, in the day of his being found guilty" (Leviticus 6:4-5).

In these offerings there is rectification in respect to God and to man, and where man is concerned the restitution must come first. This brings to mind the teaching of the Lord, "If therefore thou art offering thy gift before the altar, and there rememberest that thy brother hath aught against thee, first be reconciled to thy brother, and then come and offer thy gift" (Matthew 5:23,24). Old and New Testaments join to impress on us the importance of being right with one another, and if we fail in regard to our brother we must fail in our service toward God. Indeed the gift at the altar will not be acceptable unless we first make this restitution. Great grace at times is needed so to act, but great blessing must follow obedience to the will of the Lord in this matter.

The trespass of the one man, Adam, was not a sin of ignorance. We are told, "Adam was not beguiled, but the woman being beguiled hath fallen into transgression" (1 Timothy 2:14). With his eyes open, Adam took of the forbidden fruit and ate thereof. He knew what he was doing. "After the likeness of Adam's transgression" are these sins mentioned in the beginning of chapter 6. When a person is guilty of robbery, of oppression, of dealing falsely in the matter of a deposit, or a lost thing which he found, he usually is well aware of what he is doing. It is obvious, therefore, that we must distinguish between these and those presumptuous sins referred to in Numbers 15:30. Those were sins unto death. The divine requirement being "that soul shall be cut off from among his people"; "that soul shall be utterly cut off, his iniquity shall be upon him." Here in contrast restitution could be made, and a trespass offering resorted to, "and he shall be forgiven."

Not only was the transgressor to restore in full that wherein he had wronged his neighbour in, but he had to add the fifth part more to it. From this we note that the defrauded person or party benefited by the divine arrangement. He had more when the matter was put to rights than before he was wronged. There is something very beautiful about this, and perhaps we could consider it as connected with an aggrieved brother in our day. Instead of going the minimum length in the matter of making restitution for wrong done, we should be willing to go beyond in the spirit of adding the fifth part more.

"This is the law of the guilt offering: it is most holy. In the place where they kill the burnt offering; shall they kill the guilt offering; and the blood shall he sprinkle on the altar round about"

(Leviticus 7:1-2). Thus the guilt offering is like the sin offering - most holy. It would appear that the Lord the Spirit is taking special care in the matter to make certain regarding the holiness of these offerings. We might have been inclined to think of them differently seeing they were for sin and guilt, but they were most holy. The fat was burnt on the altar of burnt offerings, and the flesh was eaten by the males among the priest; unless, in the case of the sin offering where the blood was taken inside the holy place. But this does not apply to the trespass offering. The holiness of the trespass offerings is further indicated in that the priests who ate of them had to do so in a holy place. May we as priests in the House of God be helped to continue in that sphere and in that condition which will permit of our feeding on our great Trespass Offering!

"Stricken, smitten and afflicted,

Lo, He dies upon the tree,

'Tis the Christ by man rejected

Son of God, 'Tis He, 'Tis he!

'Tis the long-expected Saviour,

David's Son and David's Lord,

Sacrificed to show us favour

And declare the love of God.

Mark the sacrifice appointed,

See who bears the awful load;

'Tis the Word, the Lord's Anointed,

Son of Man and Son of God!

Lamb of God, for sinners wounded,

Sacrifice which cancels guilt;

None shall ever be confounded

Who on Him their hopes have built."

CHAPTER SIX: THE DRINK OFFERING (1)

The drink offering is not mentioned among the Levitical offerings of Leviticus chapters 1-7. The first significant mention of it is found in Exodus 29:40,41: "And with the one lamb a tenth part of an ephah of fine flour mingled with the fourth part of an hin of beaten oil; and the fourth part of an hin of wine for a drink offering. And the other lamb thou shalt offer at even, and shalt do thereto according to the meal offering of the morning, and according to the drink offering thereof, for a sweet savour, an offering made by fire unto the LORD."

Before dealing with the teaching on the particular occasions where it is mentioned, it is important to remember that a "drink offering" was an offering poured out in honour of the God of Israel. It consisted of wine, which speaks of joy. The psalmist says, "Wine ... maketh glad the heart of man ..." (Psalm 104:15). The responsibility of pouring out the drink offering belonged to the priests only, and was always associated with the holy place and "the place of the Name".

The heathen honoured their gods, and showed great zeal in pouring out to them their drink offerings. It was God's longing that His people should silence the reproach of the heathen by magnifying His name, and declaring His glory amongst them. The psalmist expresses it thus, "Declare His glory among the nations, His marvellous works among all the peoples. For great is the LORD, and highly to be praised. He is to be feared above all gods" (Psalm 96:3-4). What are the heathen gods? "Their idols are silver and gold, the work of men's hands" (Psalm 115:4). How sad the record of Israel's failure! Alas, they preferred to pour out libations to heathen deities. They rejected their King when they desired a king like unto other nations (1 Samuel 8:7). They rejected their God by seeking after the gods of other nations, and entering into all the wickedness associated with them.

In the Levitical offerings which have been dealt with in previous chapters, we view in type the marvellous provision of God in Christ. When the Scriptures speak of the drink offering, it is always linked with the sweet savour offerings. Thus we understand that it was always associated with a sacrifice. The drink offering was an "act" of homage to God.

In Exodus 29 a continual burnt offering was to be offered morning and evening. The day ended as it began, with a sweet savour rising unto the God of Israel, and with each of these lambs there was to be offered a fourth part of an hin of beaten oil, which was mingled in the meal offering of a tenth part of an ephah of fine flour, and a fourth part of an hin of wine. We understand an hin to be approximately six quarts and there was to be an equal portion of oil and wine.

The drink offerings had in view the time when Israel would enter into the land. The order of the offerings in Numbers 28 and 29 is most significant. In Numbers 28, we note that day by day the continual burnt offering was to be offered unto the LORD. With the continual burnt offering morning and evening was the meal offering mingled with oil, and the drink offering. In each case the measure was in accordance with the measure of Exodus 29, an equal portion of oil and wine. Thus in type a fragrance of Christ ascended Godward daily throughout the year. The psalmist perhaps had the morning sacrifice in mind when he wrote Psalm 30:5. Truly we should have the eternal morning in view as well, when this joy shall never end, and we shall join the refrain of praise to God. As we meditate on this precious thought, we might contrast our feeble praise of today with what it shall be on that blessed morrow, and consider the words of the hymn writer:

"Great God, forgive our feeble lays,

Sound out Thine own eternal praise,

A song so vast, a theme so high,

Calls for the voice that tuned the sky."

On the Sabbath, and upon feast days, a bullock, a ram and seven lambs were to be offered in accordance with the prescribed number for that specific day. Each offering was accompanied by a meal offering mingled with oil, and the drink offering. One point which stands out is the portion of drink offering for each animal. For the bullock, the largest animal to be offered, there was a half an hin of wine for a drink offering. For the ram, there was a third of an hin of wine. For the lamb, there was a quarter of an hin of wine. The priest, who continually knew that consistent joy associated with the daily morning and evening sacrifice, would no doubt come into the precious experience of overflowing with joy, and would enter into the blessed rejoicing of each event in the ceremonial life of God's people.

"Sing unto the LORD; for He hath done excellent things let this be known in all the earth. Cry aloud and shout, thou inhabitant of Zion: for great is the Holy One of Israel in the midst of thee" (Isaiah 12:5-6).

CHAPTER SEVEN: THE DRINK OFFERING (2)

"Thou shalt love the LORD thy God with all thine heart, and with all thy soul, and with all thy might" (Deuteronomy 6:5). So ran the law of God, and doubtless there would be many godly Israelites who would approximate to its requirements and sincerely love the Lord. But love must have a means of expressing itself and in Numbers chapter 15 God made provision for the freewill offerings of His people, through which they were able to express the love of their hearts and appreciation of God's goodness to them. These offerings were not compulsory. They might be brought to God's altar at any time, as prompted by the heart of the offerer. That God valued them highly we can see from the detailed provision which He made for them.

There were three classes of offerings which might be brought as a burnt offering or a peace offering and each was accompanied by a meal offering and a drink offering. If the offering was a lamb the meal offering was one-tenth part of an ephah of fine flour mingled with a quarter of a hin of oil, and the corresponding drink offering was a quarter of a hin of wine. The quantity of oil in the meal offering and wine in the drink offering increased to one-third of a hin in the case of a ram and to half a hin with a bullock. In each case the amount of oil and wine was the same. A hin measured about 3.7 litres. When the sacrifice was burning upon the altar and its sweet savour ascending to God, the drink offering was poured out upon it.

Christ as the Drink Offering

The stipulated quantity of wine was all poured out upon the altar, telling of the complete surrender of the Lord Jesus to His God and Father when "He poured out His soul unto death". "Wine that maketh glad the heart of man" speaks of joy, and doubtless in the drink offering we get a glimpse of the deep joy which the Lord Jesus experienced in the doing of His Father's will. His obedience to the Father and the joy which sprang out of it are very closely associated in His words in John 15:10,11, "If ye keep My commandments, ye shall abide in My love; even as I have kept My Father's commandments, and abide in His love. These things have I spoken unto you, that My joy may be in you, and that your joy may be fulfilled."

If His death upon the tree was His supreme act of obedience, as we understand it to be, then in that obedience His joy was full and complete. "I delight to do Thy will, O My God". It was not merely that He resigned Himself to it. No, it was something far higher than that. His holy soul delighted in it. It was His joy to do the Father's will, even when that will lead Him to the untold suffering of the Cross.

The drink offering was the final part of the freewill offering and the whole of it was made by fire unto the Lord. The fire of affliction which consumed the offering of the Lord Jesus only served to bring into clearer view His implicit obedience to His Father and the deep and holy joy which filled His soul, "who through the eternal Spirit offered Himself without blemish unto God". Like His servant who followed later, He overflowed with joy in all His affliction, and the outpouring of that joy is beautifully depicted in the pouring out of the drink offering.

Spiritual Sacrifices

Let us now consider its teaching as it concerns our offering to God when we are gathered together to worship Him. There is no doubt that the finest hour in the life of a disciple of the Lord Jesus is when in the company of God's worshipping people he partakes of the table of the Lord. "Bring an offering" said the psalmist, "and come into His courts. O worship the LORD in the beauty of holiness" (Psalm 96:8,9). Our time of worship will be greatly enriched if each one comes prepared, with some precious thoughts of Christ to offer, some fresh appreciation of His Person and worth which has been gathered in the secret place in communion with Him. As the emblems are partaken of, and Christ brought vividly before mind and heart, a deep joy fills the heart, produced by the working of the Holy Spirit. Is not this the drink offering aspect of our worship as we pour out that joy before the Lord, and "worship by the Spirit of God, and glory in Christ Jesus"? We capture something of what David had in mind when he wrote, "I will offer in His tabernacle sacrifices of joy: I will sing, yea, I will sing praises unto the LORD" (Psalm 27:6).

The offering varied according to the ability of the offerer to give. It might be a lamb that he brought to God's altar, or a ram or even a bullock, but in each case it was a freewill offering expressing his love to the Lord, and his appreciation of His goodness, and accompanying the animal was the varying amount of wine for the drink offering. Our joy in Christ will vary according to our appreciation of His worth and work, but what we have, let us pour it out unto the Lord. It will have cost us something. "Sacrifices of praise" are produced at some measure of sacrifice, and the more it costs us the more our worship will be enriched. And the more also, we believe, will God be glorified, for we remember He said, "whoso offereth the sacrifice of thanksgiving glorifieth Me" (Psalm 50:23).

Poured out as a Drink Offering

There is a third aspect of our subject to which the apostle Paul twice alludes when he refers to being himself poured out as a drink offering. From the Roman prison he wrote to Timothy, "I am already being offered (Greek: poured out as a drink offering, RV margin), and the time of my departure is come" (2 Timothy 4:6). Did he see his martyrdom approaching? Perhaps he realized that his departure would come by means of the executioner's sword and he would truly be poured out as a drink offering. But surely his words have a deeper significance than that. His whole life had been one of complete surrender to the Lord. "I will most gladly spend and be spent for your souls" he wrote to the Corinthians. Notice the gladness emphasized again. That was the character of the man. Nothing was held back. And now he was facing his final outpouring. The language he uses is significant when we remember that the final act of sacrifice was the pouring out of the drink offering upon the burnt offering and the meal offering which were already being consumed upon the altar.

There were no regrets in the heart of this spent servant; on the contrary, a deep and holy joy filled his soul. "If I am offered (Greek: poured out as a drink offering, RV margin) upon the sacrifice and service of your faith, I joy, and rejoice with you all: and in the same manner do ye also joy, and rejoice with me" (Philippians 2:17,18). The Philippian disciples in their love to the Lord had presented themselves a living sacrifice, holy, acceptable to God, and in association with this sacrifice of themselves, and as a result of it, they ministered as in priestly service, the gospel of God (see Romans 15:16). Upon their sacrifice and priestly service (for that is the meaning conveyed by the Greek word 'leitourgia') Paul now poured himself out as a drink offering. Could there be a higher expression of his love to the Lord? What a delightful contemplation as he now calls upon the Philippians to share in the joy of his outpouring.

In Paul's case it was certainly an offering made by fire unto the Lord. But he who had been shown from the beginning how many things he must suffer for His Name's sake, had learned to measure all suffering against the eternal glory which was to be revealed. "As sorrowful, yet alway rejoicing" was no vain boast on his part, and the joy of the Lord which had been his strength through all the years of his service, he continued to pour out unto the Lord until the executioner's sword transported him into His presence where there is fulness of joy and pleasures for evermore.

CHAPTER EIGHT: THE PASSOVER

The sacrifice of the Passover is not classed with the offerings of Leviticus, for it was neither a burnt-offering nor a sin-offering, nor was it burned on the altar. It was killed and roasted with fire in the homes of the people. A change took place in later years when Israel were settled in the land, for then they sacrificed the Passover at the house of God. Even then it was not offered upon the altar, though it was still roasted and eaten by the people (compare Deuteronomy 1:1-8; and also Josiah's Passover in 2 Chronicles 35).

There is something of a parallel to this in New Testament times in connection with the service of the Breaking of the Bread which is so precious to the Lord's people today, for it was first instituted by the Lord and kept by His disciples in the upper room of a man's house. Subsequently it was kept by disciples gathered in churches of God (see Acts 2:42 and 1 Corinthians 11:17-22). The Breaking of the Bread is not the function of an individual believer, or even a group of believers as such, it is the function of a church of God. See 1 Corinthians 11:18 - "When ye come together in the church".

The sacrifice of the Passover in the land of Egypt was a prerequisite to Israel's deliverance from the bondage of that land, and presents a clear type of the sacrifice of the Lord Jesus Christ who gave Himself for us that He might redeem us from the bondage of this present world, and grant us the liberty to serve God. Our authority to interpret Christ in the Passover is clearly given to us in the words of 1 Corinthians 5:7, "Our Passover also hath been sacrificed, even Christ" so we may freely study the subject with Christ in our minds.

Exodus 12 gives a detailed description of the lamb and of the two main features of the Passover, namely the sprinkling of the blood on the door, and the eating of the roast flesh. The sprinkling of the blood on the door took place on the night of deliverance from Egypt, but on subsequent Passovers there was no need for the sprinkling of the blood, though the slaying and eating of the Passover continued as a memorial feast (Exodus 12:14).

The lamb was of the first year, thus presenting a picture of undefiled innocence and purity, and foreshadowing the Person of our Lord Jesus Christ, who was unspotted from the world and unspotted by the flesh. The former is defilement from without and the latter is defilement from within. The Lord had no sinful nature within Him to cause any blemish; and at the end of His sojourn in this world He said, "The prince of the world cometh; and he hath nothing in Me" (John 14:30).

The lamb was kept from the tenth day up till the fourteenth day. This is significant, for the word 'kept' in Hebrew is the word 'shamar', which means really "to watch or to observe" and conveys to us the attitude of mind of the persons in the house as they waited those four days. It wasn't an idle "killing of time", but an industrious observation of the innocent purity of the lamb, and a contemplation of its impending death. We can imagine the effect upon them as the lamb wove its way into their affections until they felt a personal involvement in its death; especially the firstborn son, for he knew it was dying that he might live.

The Passover night is called "a night of watching (Hebrew: shamar) unto the LORD" (Exodus 12:42 RV margin) for this was not a night for sleep, but what shall we say of that night of the Saviour's sorrow in Gethsemane, when He came and found His disciples sleeping, and said unto them, "What, could ye not watch with Me one hour?" Let us ponder His night of sorrow and let us watch with Him!

The lamb was slain at even (Hebrew: between the two evenings). The expression "two evenings" is a dual word in Hebrew meaning the early and later part of the same evening, giving them a margin of some hours in which the lamb could be slain. This is the opinion of some authorities, but others think that "between the two evenings" was a specific period of time. One cannot be certain. The moment of the slaying of the lamb must have been tense, especially for the firstborn son, as he watched it being slain that he might live.

We are told in Hebrews 11:28 that the Passover was kept "by faith" but so also was the sprinkling of the blood, for it was not sufficient that the lamb had died, however grateful they may have been. They must now appropriate its death to themselves by sprinkling its blood on the doorposts and lintel of their houses, for the Lord had said, "When I see the blood, I will pass over you".

One construction put on the word 'pasach' (passover) is that of a man who is lame, who does not put his feet down regularly and in sequence, but misses a step here and there. So when the Lord was going through the land of Egypt in that night slaying the firstborn of each house, seeing the blood on the doorposts, He was caused to halt in His judgements and He passed over the door. What an arresting thought to us that God looks upon us and sees us sheltered under the blood of Christ, and He passes over us!

Inside the house the lamb was roasted with fire and eaten. This was not for their salvation, for that was secured for them by the sprinkling of the blood on the doorposts, but it was their communion, so to speak, with the lamb that had died. The effect of this "meditative" eating would be twofold - firstly, the lamb that had died was now living in them, and secondly, they would be strengthened to turn their backs upon Egypt in the morning and start out on a new life with God. It was not an eating to merely fill their stomachs. They were eating the roast flesh, but they were thinking of the lamb they had been watching for the previous few days, for this was the purpose in the eating of sacrifices. May we learn this lesson for ourselves, for we feed upon the Person of Christ so that He may be formed in us.

Eating of the sacrifice speaks of communion with the sacrifice and eating of it roast with fire speaks of communion with its sufferings. This is what will enable the disciple of Christ to turn his back on the things of this world, and will deliver him from its bondage. As he feeds himself on Christ's sufferings not only is Christ formed in him, but, like Christ Himself, he will overcome the world. The Israelites ate the Passover with bitter herbs, to impart to them a "lingering" taste or a lasting memory, and with unleavened or unsweetened bread, which could not affect the taste of the bitter herbs, for unleavened bread is tasteless to the natural appetite.

What practical lessons abound in these things for disciples of our Lord Jesus Christ We gladly do as they did that night - put on the character of those who are ready to leave, for they had their loins girded, shoes on their feet, and staff in their hand. The internal change they experienced as they fed upon the roast lamb was to have external manifestation in their deportment as pilgrims and strangers in the land.

The effect of the eating of the roast lamb was the building up within them of a resistance to the land in which they had been in bondage so long. The disciple of Christ today must build up a similar resistance by his feeding in communion on his Passover, for if he does not feed on Christ, he will not go very far on the Christian pathway.

"'Tis we, O God, whom Thou hast shown

The deadly bitterness of sin

We, who forgiving love have known

May fitly bring thank-offerings in.

Thy presence called for Israel's praise

Encompassed by their mortal foes;

And when in death they met their gaze

What songs of glorious triumph rose!

And we have known redemption, Lord

From bondage worse than theirs by far;

Sin held us by a stronger cord,

Yet by thy mercy free we are!

The blest Redeemer's groans and tears,

His death the power of darkness broke;

Bursting the chains we wore for years,

He freed us from the iron yoke.

Divine Deliverer! He alone

Thy people from the deep could bring;

The glorious triumph all His own,

His name, His might, His grace we sing!"

CHAPTER NINE: THE RED HEIFER

The slaying and burning of the red heifer was God's provision for the defilement of death. The Israelite who came into contact with a dead person became defiled. Sometimes many were so affected. It is significant that the statute relative to the red heifer, in Numbers 19, was given after Israel refused to enter the land. Death claimed all the fighting men save two.

The ashes of the heifer with living water, described as "a water of separation," when sprinkled upon the defiled on the appointed days wrought cleansing. In Hebrews 9 we have defilement through dead works; from such defilement the blood of Christ can cleanse the conscience. The red heifer was a sin offering. It must be a heifer upon which never came a yoke, and it must be without blemish. It was slain outside the camp and was witnessed by Eleazar, the priest. "One shall slay her before his face ... and one shall burn the heifer in his sight." (Please read Acts 10:41 and 1 Peter 5:1.) With his finger he took the blood, and sprinkled it toward the front of the tent of meeting seven times.

The shadow or type in the burning of the red heifer will help us to enter into the spirit of the words in Psalm 22, "My heart is like wax; It is melted in the midst of My bowels ... Thou hast brought Me into the dust (ashes) of death." The character of the fire in the burnt offering was of a slower kind and it rather fed upon the offering as if with delight. When the sacrifice was fully subjected to the fierce heat, cedar wood, hyssop and scarlet (wool) were cast into the midst of the burning. Each of these in some way added virtue and worth to the sacrifice. Yet, we sing truly, "All are too mean to speak His worth, Too mean to set the Saviour forth."

Cedar wood points to the humanity of the Lord Jesus; in this case it probably speaks of His excellencies as a Man (see Matthew 8:27; Luke 7:16, 9.48). In the eyes of enlightened ones, "His aspect is like Lebanon, excellent as the cedars" (Song of Songs 5:15). The fact that men totally failed to recognize His glorious worth, and finally gave to Him the very lowest place, only serve to enhance His beauty, for sure we are that as God beheld Him upon the Cross, none of the cedar-like excellence of His Manhood was affected by the shameful tree. At Calvary the cedar was cast into the midst of the burning: there men confessed, "He saved others." It was there He reached the dying robber, and many myriads besides.

The place given to hyssop in the Bible indicates that it speaks of faith. So very different from the strong and majestic cedar, this little plant grew by clinging to the wall (1 Kings 4:33), aptly foreshadowing the One who, belonging originally to heights far, far above Lebanon, condescended to fill a little place, being made to trust upon His mother's breast (Psalm 22:9). The world was made by Him, the heavens are the work of His fingers, and yet He was meek and lowly, and was led as a Lamb to the slaughter. In reproach, His enemies witnessed of Him in the utter loneliness of the Cross, "He trusted in God." Truly the hyssop was cast into the midst of the burning, and sweet and real were the psalmist's words of Christ at that time, "Thou wilt not leave My soul in Sheol." What acceptance such faith would find with God!

So truly did the Saviour become sin for us that His inward experience is reflected in the words, "I am a Worm, and no man, a reproach of men, and despised of the people" (Psalm 22:6). This may be an answer to the scarlet (worm scarlet) which Eleazar used in conjunction with the cedar and the hyssop. Scarlet may speak of the kingship of Christ, for He died with this title over His head, yes, and He was crowned as well, but He was bruised (crushed) for our iniquities. The climax of the impressive type outside the camp of Israel was the gathering and the carrying-away of the ashes (dust). Psalm 22:15 has the same word; these ashes differ from the altar ashes which properly were fatty ashes, but the ashes of Numbers 19 might have been blown away with the wind. What a tragic end the Cross was to such a noble life, which would no glory borrow, no majesty from earth! To those sad men and women who loved Him to the end, His death left them with what seemed to some, no doubt, a mere handful of ashes, what remained of hope in their breasts seemed liable to be blown away.

We cannot enter into His thoughts as He felt His strength being dried up like a potsherd, but His simple faith never failed; with them it was different; they were slow to believe what the prophets had spoken. Joseph and Nicodemus, clean men, carried the precious body away, like the ashes of old, and in this wondrous death there is power to separate, to cleanse souls from death and this defiling world. The ashes in Numbers 19 were laid up in a clean place, so that when any in Israel were defiled this means of cleansing was available.

Where there was neglect (verse 18), or disregard (verse 20), the unclean brought defilement upon others, indeed upon the sanctuary of the Lord. That soul was cut off from Israel. But even such as did submit themselves to the statute affected others, for whatever or whoever came into contact with the unclean person also became unclean, to the very one who touched the water. How serious this matter is in this day of the substance, compared with that of the shadow! If a man defiled the dwelling place of God by having made contact with the bone of a man, and remained uncleansed, should we not be more alive to the defiling influences of this unclean world? Hebrews 9 sums it up under the expression of "dead works" and serious is the effect of such upon an enlightened conscience, if it remains uncleansed by the blood of Christ.

There is a point worth noting in verse 15, where we read of open vessels with no covering bound upon them being made unclean by death. How suggestive this is of the need to keep ourselves unspotted from the world, to gird up the loins of the mind, and to exercise increasing care as to that to which we lend our ears. Perhaps there is no season when the effects of defilement trouble us so much as on the Lord's day in our most holy exercises, when the mind should be free from such distraction. In conclusion we turn in thought to the Song of Songs where the words are found: "A garden shut up is my sister, my bride a spring shut up, a fountain sealed" (4:12). "It is the voice of my beloved that knocketh, saying, "Open to me ... my undefiled" (5:2).

CHAPTER TEN: THE MEANING TO CHRISTIANS TODAY

When we consider the offerings, we find a suggestive outline of what might be termed our way of approach. God commences with the burnt offering and moves onward to the trespass offering, but in our experience we seem to make contact firstly with the trespass offering. Conviction of sin, through the working of the Holy Spirit, had to do especially with acts of trespass. As the sense of guilt burdened us we longed for the assurance of divine forgiveness, and great was our joy when our eyes were opened to realize that Christ was delivered up for our trespasses, and was raised for our justification.

A further exercise was experienced when we became conscious that we were not without failure and guilt in our lives after having been saved. Then it was exceedingly precious to learn that the blood of Jesus cleanses us from all sin. It is then, as it were, that we can advance to enjoy Christ as our peace offering - He who made peace through the blood of His cross. With these forming a basis for our faith and joy we can advance to consider the moral glories of the Man Christ Jesus as set out in type in the meal offering. We are assured that a right understanding of the Person of Christ is not obtainable where the above progress is lacking; but wonderful is the joy occasioned from contemplation of what He is, and what He accomplished, as set out in these shadows.

Then last of all, and as arriving at a zenith, we reach the burnt offering, which, as we have shown, shadows Christ as giving Himself to God, and accomplishing all the will of God. Here we wish to express a note of warning. Some assert that when we approach God in priestly service on the Lord's day morning at the Remembrance of our Lord Jesus and give Him our spiritual sacrifices, that these should be in the burnt offering aspect of His death only. This we judge is a mistaken view. We should wave Christ before God in every aspect of His precious Person and work - the work He wrought for us in His death and resurrection. The great atoning work which He accomplished at Calvary has many facets, and the burnt offering is but one of the many. We must be free to present the whole before God as the blessed Holy Spirit may direct. God's delight is great in every aspect of the work of His Son upon the cross.

May it be that our consideration of the offerings will be used of God in such a way that priestly service in the holies may be increasingly a joy to Him upon whom we call as the God and Father of our Lord Jesus Christ! "That with one accord ye may with one mouth glorify the God and Father of our Lord Jesus Christ."

CHAPTER ELEVEN: THE SWEET SAVOUR OF CHRIST

The first reference to a sweet savour is found in Genesis 8:20-22 and the word "sweet" (Hebrew: "pleasant") is derived from another word which means "to rest or settle down." The name of Noah ("quiet or rest") is another derivative of that Hebrew word. The blessings of rest are prominent in the Scriptures, whether it be the rest which God enjoyed after the six days of His creative work or whether it is in the commandment concerning the Sabbath.

The Christian comes to the Lord and finds peace and rest, and the thought is prominently associated with the house of God; especially is it dealt with in Hebrews 4. The enjoyment of rest, and acts which are in accordance with it, go up to God as a sweet savour. He delights to see His people manifesting their appreciation of the rest which is His in Christ and which is ours in Christ, and especially when such things are expressed by those in the house of God where rest finds its highest expression on earth, for those who find themselves there can devote themselves to doing the will of God in full priestly service which is in accordance with His will.

Noah, after many years among men of a wicked generation, was found righteous before God and taken away to be the first of a new generation. The sins of earth had been dealt with by the Flood, and when Noah returned to solid earth it was as to a newly cleansed place. There was in it no hindrance to his offering up to God an expression of thanks and of adoration in a burnt-offering. "And the LORD smelled the sweet savour" (Genesis 5: 21).

It was a thing so precious to God that at the outset there was set forth in type the rest and quietness of a new creation and He entered into a covenant that He would not again smite every thing living, as He had done. We little know the value of giving to God anything which today is accounted by Him as a sweet-savour offering. We are a new creation in Christ and, like Noah, can offer up the token of a devoted life. That devotion must be associated with the highest example of devotion as seen in the Lord Jesus Christ. We are accepted in the Beloved Son, and any offerings of human lives and lips are accepted when they have shown something of Christ.

Coming now to the words heading this chapter, they are found in a remarkable setting in 2 Corinthians 2:15, and analogous words are found in Ephesians 5:2. Verses 1 and 2 of Ephesians 5 are sandwiched between two passages of Scripture which are of solemn teaching, for in Ephesians 4:25-32 we have things said which remind us of the days of Noah, and in Ephesians 5 we are reminded of despicable things which can be found even among Christians. Between these two sombre passages we might have expected to hear of Christ the Sin-offering, but instead we get the lovely thought of Christ as an Offering of a sweet savour. A people among whom are things such as related in Ephesians 4 could be deserving of the utmost wrath of God, but the grieving of the Holy Spirit is not here judged as it was in the days of Noah. Sweet influences are brought to bear.

"Let all bitterness, and wrath, and anger, and clamour, and railing, be put away from you, with all malice: and be ye kind one to another, tender-hearted, forgiving each other, even as God also in Christ forgave you" (Ephesians 4:31-32).

He is a man of exceptional experience among Christians who has not known the need for some such exhortation and one wishes that more heed were given to it. Human nature comes out in works such as those referred to, but the Christian is exhorted to become an imitator of God, and to walk in love, after the manner of Christ, so that his works and life are offered to God in the Name of the Lord Jesus. If this were done by all believers earth would become heavenly in character, at least in that portion of it wherein there is Christian love and fellowship.

Then in 2 Corinthians 2 we find the apostle Paul writing of his work towards the unsaved and of his ministrations to the saved in the church of God in Corinth. Here again Christian forgiveness is touched upon: "To whom ye forgive anything, I forgive also: for what I also have forgiven, if I have forgiven anything, for your sakes have I forgiven it in the Person of Christ" (2 Corinthians 2:10). Then He touches upon another side of the matter, for Satan would have us to hug our unforgiving natures and even would whisper words in our ears to suggest reasons why we should not forgive. Let saints realize that sometimes reluctance to forgive is due to a direct assault by Satan upon believers, and often he comes as if he were an angel of light instead of darkness, but the light is a false light, and well might Paul say, that forgiveness should be exercised, "that no advantage may be gained over us by Satan: for we are not ignorant of his devices" (2 Corinthians 2:11).

Paul's heart was so burdened by this matter that though there had been a door opened for the proclamation of the gospel in Troas he felt that he had to leave Troas because he was anxious about the Corinthians, and when he receives the good news from Titus he gives expression to the remarkable words, "But thanks be unto God, which always leadeth us in triumph in Christ, and maketh manifest through us the savour of His knowledge in every place. For we are a sweet savour of Christ unto God, in them that are being saved, and in them that are perishing" (2 Corinthians 2:14-15).

So we see how closely he links the two matters, right relationship between saints, and the proclaiming the gospel of God. As said previously we little know the blessing that can come from the offering up of a sweet savour of Christ, and it will be well for us to ponder the effect of a lack of forgiveness among saints on the proclamation of the gospel.

"Sweet is the savour of His name,

Who suffered in His people's stead

His portion here reproach and shame

He liveth now, He once was dead!"

CHAPTER TWELVE: NO SWEETNESS!

Some fruits look delicious but cause disappointment when eaten, as they can turn out to be dry and totally lacking in sweetness. Israel's God looked forward to enjoying the worship that would arise from the hearts of those He had personally set free from slavery and brought into a close relationship with Himself. What joy was His when the fire was first set alight on the copper altar in the wilderness! The people also rejoiced in the privilege of participating in the service of God. The fragrance that ascended from the various offerings in those early days however, lost its savour to God in succeeding generations.

God looked for much, but was greatly disappointed by the attitude of the nation to His will and by their dealings with one another. They were often referred to as the fig tree, but the fruit they yielded throughout the centuries proved to be unpleasant, until finally, God caused them to be carried away into captivity. Before this captivity took place the prophet Isaiah conveyed to the men of his day a cry from the heart of God, "Thou hast bought me no sweet cane with honey, neither hast thou filled me with the fat of thy sacrifices" (Isaiah 43:24). These two ingredients, the fat and the sweet cane, seem to be linked together in the context of worship (vv.21,23).

The fat of all the offerings was without exception God's portion (Leviticus 3:16, 7:23). It spoke of an aspect of the person of the coming Son that only God could fully appreciate. The sweet cane or calamus was one of the substances found in the holy anointing oil of Exodus 30:23, but God was missing this ingredient in the service of His people, and because of its absence their worship lacked sweetness. The challenge comes to our hearts today

- are we lacking in our service to God? Do the sacrifices that we offer in our capacity as a holy priesthood contain the sweetness which God through the Spirit can delight in (Psalm 22:3)?

The verse in Isaiah reads, "Thou hast bought me no sweet cane". What was the problem? In a word, cost. They were unwilling to part with something, and that resulted in God being robbed of His portion. We also must pay the price to make our worship acceptable to God. It will cost us time to sit with the Word, meditating upon it and allowing the Holy Spirit to warm our hearts with precious thoughts of the person and work of Christ. There are many things that consume our time, some legitimate, others not so legitimate. One of the greatest dangers lies in what has been referred to as the "plug-in drug" namely, television, which if uncontrolled, can seriously affect the believer's appetite for the Word.

If many responsible bodies in our day are concerned about the effects of so much viewing, should not those who own Christ as Lord see to it that the influence of television does not dominate the free time in home life? There are also things that might be allowed to creep into our personal relationships which would hinder our worship. One cannot give acceptable worship to God from a heart that is not at peace with one's neighbour. Paul, writing to the Ephesians, gave the following exhortation: "Let all bitterness, and wrath, and anger, and clamour, and railing, be put away from you, with all malice: and be ye kind one to another, tender-hearted, forgiving each other, even as God also in Christ forgave you" (Ephesians 4:31,32).

Such an attitude of mind should characterize us in our dealings with one another. Disruption of relationships is a breeding ground for bitterness which can completely dry up the exercise of free worship (Hebrews 12:15), and rob it of its sweetness. As the people of God we have a unique privilege and responsibility that as a holy priesthood we might offer worship, from grateful and pure hearts that respond to the full provision we have in our Lord Jesus Christ.

CHAPTER THIRTEEN: OFFERINGS IN THE MILLENNIAL KINGDOM

It is evident from the Scriptures that there will indeed be a temple in Jerusalem during the thousand years when the Lord Jesus Christ will exercise His rule and authority over this world. Such a passage as Isaiah 2:2-4, is clearly millennial in its context because of the words of verse 4, "and they shall beat their swords into plowshares, and their spears into pruning hooks: nation shall not lift up sword against nation, neither shall they learn war any more". This being so, the words of the previous verses, which refer to the house of God, must refer to that house in millennial times.

When the peoples shall say, "Come ye, and let us go up to the mountain of the LORD, to the house of the God of Jacob", they will manifest a true change of heart in that they themselves offer willingly to go up. This willingness is also seen in the use of the word "flow" in verse 2, "all nations shall flow unto it", for there is no thought of pressure or compulsion in the word "flow". It speaks of water finding its own level and coming to rest, just as men of all times find their rest in God.

The mountain of the Lord's house will be firmly established at the head of the mountains. This may have reference to physical changes in the earth, as described in the 46th Psalm, which will take place as a result of the earthquakes prior to the coming of the Son of Man, but more important than this is the fact that the house of the Lord in Jerusalem will be established in fame and reputation as the place where men may go to learn the knowledge of the Lord. There is no higher knowledge than this; it is greater than all the sciences, and many peoples will say, "Come ye, and let us go up to the mountain of the LORD, to the house of the God of Jacob; and He will teach us of His ways, and we will walk in His paths: for out of Zion shall go forth the law, and the word of the LORD from Jerusalem". The Lord will sit as Judge, and will decide the controversies of nations with decisions of perfect righteousness against which there is no appeal, for there is no higher court. All nations will benefit from the administration of the Righteous Judge, for out of Zion will go forth the law, and the word of the Lord from Jerusalem.

When we consider the material consequences of the cessation of all wars, and the subsequent channelling of wealth into the produce of the earth, and into rebuilding programmes, we can imagine the wealth of the nations that will be poured into Israel, as mentioned in Isaiah 60:5, "the wealth of the nations shall come unto thee". Israel's sons also shall come from afar, bringing their silver and their gold with them for the name of the Lord their God and for the Holy One of Israel (v.9). Out of this abundance of wealth Israel will build a temple of magnificence and glory such as men have never seen before. The Lord Himself speaks of it with affection as, "My beautiful house" (v.7) or "the house of My glory", for the house will be built for the habitation of His glory.

In those days Israel will know the Lord Jesus Christ as their Redeemer, and as their King, for the veil of unbelief will be removed from their hearts, and they will give vent to their feelings of gratitude and appreciation in the vast material offerings which they will bring for the building of the temple. The Lord will make the entire city of Jerusalem an eternal excellency, a joy of many generations, and men shall call her, the city of the Lord, the Zion of the Holy One of Israel (Isaiah 60:14-15).

What a transformation will be seen in the hearts of men when they come to Jerusalem to minister to Israel, and to seek the favour of Israel's God! The house of God will be called a house of prayer for all peoples, and they will offer burnt-offerings and sacrifices with acceptance upon the altar of the Lord (Isaiah 56:7). Note in this verse that the Lord will make them joyful in His house of prayer. Isn't this as it should be? The service of God's house, whether it be sacrifice or prayer, ought to be a service of great joy, and if that joy is lacking, we are lacking in our strength to serve Him, even as Nehemiah said, "The joy of the LORD is your strength". It is the desire of God that men should serve Him and worship Him with joyful hearts, and in those millennial days it will be the crowning joy of men's hearts to go up to the house of God in Jerusalem.

The question has often been raised as to the purpose of sacrifice and offering in millennial times, in view of the fact that since the sacrifice of our Lord Jesus Christ, there is no more offering for sin. One of the major themes dealt with in the epistle to the Hebrews is the truth of the once-for-all Sacrifice through which we have obtained eternal redemption. Why then should God accept sacrifices and offerings again as in Old Testament times? for they shall come up with acceptance upon His altar (Isaiah 60:7; 56:7). God accepted the sacrifices of Old Testament times because they were a sweet savour to Him of the coming sacrifice of His Son. Could He not then accept those millennial sacrifices as being a sweet memorial of the sacrifice of His beloved Son, especially as those who will minister the sacrifices will be circumcised in heart as well as in flesh? (Ezekiel 44:9). There will be no hypocrisy in that service as there was in so many in Israel in the past, but rather a heartfelt appreciation of the spiritual significance of what they are doing. The Levites of that day will be purged and purified by the furnace of affliction, and they will offer unto the Lord offerings in righteousness (Malachi 3:3), thus adding character to the joyful service of God's house.

The temple described by Ezekiel in chapters 40-46 has not been built yet. He was given the vision of this house while he was a captive in Babylon, then sixty-five years later the remnant went up from Babylon to Jerusalem, to rebuild the temple which a great king of Israel built many years before (Ezra 5:11); this, of course, being Solomon's temple. Ezekiel is describing a temple greater in extent than that which Solomon built, and is obviously suited to the days of Israel's glory during the reign of our Lord Jesus Christ.

The view that the Ezekiel temple was an alternative plan of God would conflict with the fact that Solomon's temple was God's plan (with certain modifications) for the remnant who were in captivity with Ezekiel. We are thus led to the conclusion that the Ezekiel temple is millennial, and is the house of the God of Jacob referred to in the passage in Isaiah quoted earlier in this chapter. The sons of Zadok will be given the priesthood as a recompense for their faithfulness in keeping the charge of God's sanctuary in days when Israel went astray from the Lord, and one of their prime duties will be to teach God's people the difference between the holy and the common (Ezekiel 44:23). The reason for this is given in the previous chapter, where the Lord emphasizes the fact that the house was the place of His throne, and the place of the soles of His feet, where He would rest in the midst of the children of Israel (43:7). But Israel had no respect or reverence for the holy character of the Lord their God, and we read that they set their threshold by His threshold, and their doorpost by His doorpost, and there was but the wall between Him and them. All this indicates a lowering of spiritual standards, and a low appreciation of the holiness of their God, who plainly told them, "Ye shall reverence My sanctuary!" When the Lord said, "There was but the wall between Me and them", we realize what a thin line of separation the people observed between the holy and the common. Let us not fall into this snare in our day and time, and cause Him the grief that He suffered in Israel's day, for God is holy and His dwelling-place is holy.

Ezekiel describes a very large courtyard, approximately one mile square, in the centre of which is the temple building itself, thus giving the impression of the sanctified distinction of that holy dwelling-place. It is difficult to follow the wording of Ezekiel's description of the temple building, but there are evidently two compartments, similar to the tabernacle, and Solomon's temple. The first is called the temple, and the second the most holy place (Ezekiel 41:4), being divided by two swinging doors as in Solomon's temple. It seems strange that there is no mention of the ark of the covenant, or a lampstand or table of shewbread. Will these things all have fulfilled their purpose as types, and be superseded by the real Presence of the Lord? The altar of burnt-offering is retained, and given prominence in its place in the courtyard, "before the house". God calls this altar "His table" (Ezekiel 41.22; 44.16), for it is the place where He will share with His people the precious memorial of the sacrifice of His beloved Son. What a privilege will be given to the sons of Zadok of whom the Lord says, "They shall come near to My table"!

The feast of the Passover will be observed in those days (chapter 45) but the priest will first offer a sin-offering, then take of its blood and put it upon the doorposts of the house of God. What a significant memorial to God, who gave the instruction to Israel in the land of Egypt to put the blood on the doorposts of their houses and said, "When I see the blood, I will pass over you"! One wonders what the Lord Jesus Christ meant when He said to His disciples in the upper room, "I will not eat it (the Passover) until it be fulfilled in the kingdom of God" (Luke 22:16). Will He participate in some way in the great seven-day festival of burnt-offerings which will be the millennial Passover?

Then there will be the joyful festival of tabernacles in the seventh month, when the nation of Israel will remember all their sojournings and wanderings throughout the world, but will rejoice in the goodness of their God who has brought them home. This will be Israel's joy, but all the nations will be commanded by Israel's God to come to Jerusalem and rejoice with them, and to worship the Lord God of Israel. If they do not come, the Lord will withhold the rain from them, and send a plague upon them (Zechariah 14:16-19). The city of Jerusalem in those days will be renowned throughout the world, but her chief renown will be that she will be called, "Jehovah-shammah" – "The LORD is there" (Ezekiel 48:35).

ABOUT THE AUTHORS – VOLUME TWO

CHAPTER ONE: GEORGE PRASHER

CHAPTER TWO: GEORGE PRASHER

CHAPTER THREE: GEORGE PRASHER

CHAPTER FOUR: GEORGE PRASHER

CHAPTER FIVE: GEORGE PRASHER

CHAPTER SIX: FRED LUNDWILL

CHAPTER SEVEN: ALAN TOMS

CHAPTER EIGHT: GEORGE PRASHER

CHAPTER NINE: H. BRINDLE

CHAPTER TEN: HARRY KING

CHAPTER ELEVEN: DR A.T. DOODSON

CHAPTER TWELVE: IAN LITHGOW

CHAPTER THIRTEEN: HARRY KING

Did you love *The Hidden Christ: Offerings and Sacrifices*? Then you should read *Called As We Are* by Ed Neely!

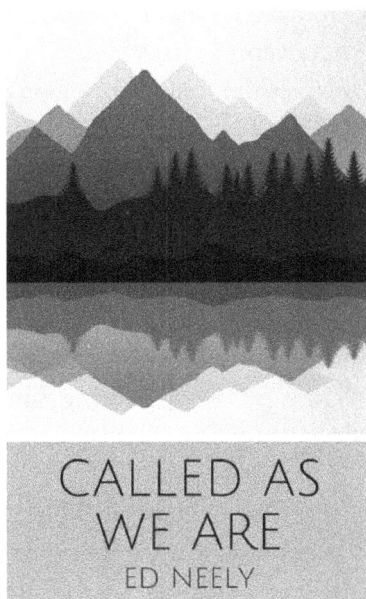

This collection of writings by Bible teacher and evangelist Ed Neely cover a wide range of topics for all Christians today - holy living, giving, worship, prayer and witnessing, with a special focus on exploring God's purposes for individuals and disciples called together.

Also by Hayes Press

The Road Through Calvary: 40 Devotional Readings
Lovers of God's House
Different Discipleship: Jesus' Sermon on the Mount
No Time for Apathy
The House of God: Past, Present and Future
The Kingdom of God
Knowing God: His Names and Nature
Needed Truth 1888-1988: A Centenary Review of Major Themes
Churches of God: Their Constitution and Functions
Collected Writings On ... Exploring Biblical Fellowship
Collected Writings On ... Exploring Biblical Hope
Collected Writings On ... The Cross of Christ
Builders for God
Collected Writings On ... Exploring Biblical Faithfulness
Collected Writings On ... Exploring Biblical Joy
Possessing the Land: Spiritual Lessons from Joshua
Collected Writings On ... Exploring Biblical Holiness
Collected Writings On ... Exploring Biblical Faith
Collected Writings On ... Exploring Biblical Love
These Three Remain...Exploring Biblical Faith, Hope and Love
The Teaching and Testimony of the Apostles
Pressure Points - Biblical Advice for 20 of Life's Biggest Challenges
The Exalted One - 12 Portraits of Christ
The Faith: Outlines of Scripture Doctrine
Elders and the Elderhood: In Principle, In Practice
Is There a Purpose to Life?
Bible Covenants 101
The Hidden Christ: Offerings and Sacrifices

About the Publisher

Hayes Press (www.hayespress.org) is a registered charity in the United Kingdom, whose primary mission is to disseminate the Word of God, mainly through literature. It is one of the largest distributors of gospel tracts and leaflets in the United Kingdom, with over 100 titles and hundreds of thousands despatched annually.

Hayes Press also publishes Plus Eagles Wings, a fun and educational Bible magazine for children, six times a year and Golden Bells, a popular daily Bible reading calendar in wall or desk formats.

Also available are over 100 Bibles in many different versions, shapes and sizes, Christmas cards, Christian jewellery, Eikos Bible Art, Bible text posters and much more!

www.ingramcontent.com/pod-product-compliance
Lightning Source LLC
Chambersburg PA
CBHW060658030426
42337CB00017B/2672